5

2

6

BEGINNER'S GUIDE RIPPLES FOR BABY

Want an easy-to-crochet baby gift that will make a grand impression? Then this **beginner's guidebook** is just for you — **the ripple is one of the simplest patterns you can make!** And this appealing array of **8 baby-pleasing designs** has the perfect afghan to welcome the newcomer in style. Our **clear instructions** and **full-color photographs** are so inspiring and user-friendly, you'll refer to this little volume again and again when other New Arrivals come along.

HOW IS THE RIPPLE PATTERN CREATED?

You will be amazed at the simplicity of the ripple pattern. We've broken it into 3 easy steps. Take a look—

MAKE THE CHAIN. All ripple afghans, no matter how simple or intricate looking, begin with a crocheted chain.

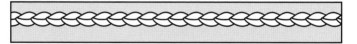

USE INCREASES AND DECREASES TO ESTABLISH THE PATTERN. The first row starts the ripple pattern with evenly spaced increases and decreases. This creates the up and down pattern.

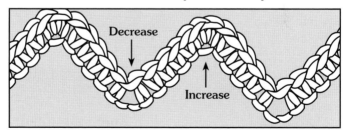

CONTINUE THE ESTABLISHED PATTERN TO CREATE THE RIPPLE. Every row is the same with the increases and decreases "stacked" over each other. Once you learn the pattern, you can work the ripple without even referring back to the instructions.

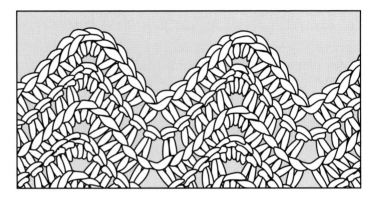

TRY IT YOURSELF!

Now that you have the concept, pick up some worsted weight yarn and a size H hook and let's try a swatch with a simple single crochet ripple.

Chain 66 loosely.

Work Row 1: Sc in third ch from hook and in next 4 chs, 3 sc in next ch *(this creates the "peak" of the ripple)*, ★ sc in next 5 chs, skip next 2 chs *(this creates the "valley" of the ripple)*, sc in next 5 chs, 3 sc in next ch; repeat from ★ across to last 6 chs, sc in last 6 chs: 66 sc.

Work Rows 2-8: Ch 1, turn; working in Back Loops Only, skip first 2 sc, sc in next 5 sc, 3 sc in next sc *("peak")*, ★ sc in next 5 sc, skip next 2 sc *("valley")*, sc in next 5 sc, 3 sc in next sc; repeat from ★ across to last 6 sc, sc in last 6 sc.

Finish off.

Congratulations! You did it. Now pick one of our inspiring patterns and your favorite yarn and get started on your very own ripple afghan.

1. RAINBOW IN THE CLOUDS

Shown on Front Cover.

Finished Size:
36" x 45"

MATERIALS
Sport Weight Yarn:
White - 9$^1/_2$ ounces,
(270 grams, 1,010 yards)
Blue - 2$^3/_4$ ounces,
(80 grams, 290 yards)
Lavender - 2 ounces,
(60 grams, 215 yards)
Yellow - 2 ounces,
(60 grams, 215 yards)
Pink - 2 ounces,
(60 grams, 215 yards)
Crochet hook, size G (4.00 mm)
or size needed for gauge

GAUGE: In pattern, from point
to point = 7$^1/_4$"; 8 rows = 4$^1/_4$"

COLOR SEQUENCE
Work one row **each**: (Blue,
White) twice, ★ (Lavender,
White) twice, (Yellow, White)
twice, (Pink, White) twice, (Blue,
White) twice; repeat from ★ 4
times **more**.

AFGHAN BODY
With Blue, ch 179 **loosely**, place
marker in third ch from hook for
st placement.

*To work decrease (uses next 2
sts),* YO, insert hook in same st
as last st made, YO and pull up
a loop, YO and draw through 2
loops on hook, YO, skip next st,
insert hook in next st, YO and
pull up a loop, YO and draw
through 2 loops on hook, YO
and draw through all 3 loops on
hook **(counts as one dc)**.

*To work double decrease
(uses next 4 sts),* YO, insert
hook in same st as last st made,
YO and pull up a loop, YO and
draw through 2 loops on hook,
★ YO, skip **next** st, insert hook
in **next** st, YO and pull up a loop,
YO and draw through 2 loops on
hook; repeat from ★ once **more**,
YO and draw through all 4 loops
on hook **(counts as one dc)**.

Row 1 (Right side)**:** Dc in fifth
ch from hook, (ch 1, decrease) 6
times, ch 1, dc in same ch as last
st made, (ch 1, decrease, ch 1,
dc in same ch as last st made)
twice, ★ (ch 1, decrease) 5 times,
(ch 1, double decrease) 3 times,
(ch 1, decrease) 5 times, ch 1, dc
in same ch as last st made, (ch 1,
decrease, ch 1, dc in same ch as
last st made) twice; repeat from
★ 3 times **more**, (ch 1, decrease)
7 times; finish off: 91 dc and 90
chs.

Note: Mark last row as **right**
side.

To work Puff St, ch 2, ★ YO, insert hook in back ridge of second ch from hook *(Fig. 2c, page 22)*, YO and pull up a loop; repeat from ★ once **more**, YO and draw through all 5 loops on hook.

Row 2: With **wrong** side facing and working in Front Loops Only *(Fig. 9, page 23)*, join White with sc in first dc *(see Joining With Sc, page 23)*; ★ work Puff St, skip next ch, sc in next dc; repeat from ★ across; finish off: 91 sc and 90 Puff Sts.

To work beginning double decrease (uses next 4 sts), ch 2, ★ YO, skip **next** Puff St, insert hook in **next** sc, YO and pull up a loop, YO and draw through 2 loops on hook; repeat from ★ once **more**, YO and draw through all 3 loops on hook **(counts as one dc)**.

Row 3: With **right** side facing and working in Back Loops Only, join next color with slip st in first sc; work beginning double decrease, (ch 1, decrease) 6 times, ch 1, dc in same sc as last st made, (ch 1, decrease, ch 1, dc in same sc as last st made) twice, ★ (ch 1, decrease) 5 times, (ch 1, double decrease) 3 times, (ch 1, decrease) 5 times, ch 1, dc in same sc as last st made, (ch 1, decrease, ch 1, dc in same sc as last st made) twice; repeat from ★ 3 times **more**, (ch 1, decrease) 6 times, ch 1, double decrease; finish off: 91 dc and 90 chs.

Row 4: With **wrong** side facing and working in Front Loops Only, join White with sc in first dc; ★ work Puff St, skip next ch, sc in next dc; repeat from ★ across; finish off: 91 sc and 90 Puff Sts.

Rows 5-84: Repeat Rows 3 and 4, 40 times; at end of Row 84, do **not** finish off.

EDGING
With **wrong** side facing, sc evenly across end of rows; working in free loops of beginning ch *(Fig. 10, page 23)*, sc in marked ch, ★ work Puff St, skip next ch, sc in next ch; repeat from ★ across; sc evenly across end of rows; join with slip st to first sc on Row 84, finish off.

Design by Tammy Kreimeyer.

2. GENTLE BREEZE

Shown on Back Cover.

Finished Size:
34" x 45"

MATERIALS
Sport Weight Yarn:
15½ ounces,
(440 grams, 1,645 yards)
Crochet hook, size G (4.00 mm)
or size needed for gauge

GAUGE: In pattern, from point to point = 3"; 5 rows = 3¼"

AFGHAN BODY
Ch 190 **loosely.**

Row 1 (Right side): Dc in fifth ch from hook, ch 1, skip next ch, (dc in next ch, ch 1, skip next ch) twice, 3 dc in next ch, ch 3, 3 dc in next ch, ch 1, (skip next ch, dc in next ch, ch 1) twice, ★ (YO, skip **next** ch, insert hook in **next** ch, YO and pull up a loop, YO and draw through 2 loops on hook) 3 times, YO and draw through all 4 loops on hook, ch 1, skip next ch, (dc in next ch, ch 1, skip next ch) twice, 3 dc in next ch, ch 3, 3 dc in next ch, ch 1, (skip next ch, dc in next ch, ch 1) twice; repeat from ★ across to last 4 chs, (YO, skip **next** ch, insert hook in **next** ch, YO and pull up a loop, YO and draw through 2 loops on hook) twice, YO and draw through all 3 loops on hook: 122 sts and 77 sps.

To work Cluster, YO, insert hook in next dc, YO and pull up a loop, YO and draw through 2 loops on hook, YO twice, skip next ch-1 sp, insert hook in next st, YO and pull up a loop, (YO and draw through 2 loops on hook) twice, ★ YO twice, insert hook in **same** st, YO and pull up a loop, (YO and draw through 2 loops on hook) twice; repeat from ★ 2 times **more**, YO, insert hook in next dc, YO and pull up a loop, YO and draw through 2 loops on hook, YO and draw through all 7 loops on hook. Push Cluster to **right** side.

To work ending decrease (uses next 2 dc), ★ YO, insert hook in **next** dc, YO and pull up a loop, YO and draw through 2 loops on hook; repeat from ★ once **more**, YO and draw through all 3 loops on hook.

Row 2: Ch 2, turn; skip first st, (dc in next dc, ch 1) 3 times, (3 dc, ch 3, 3 dc) in next ch-3 sp, ch 1, skip next 2 dc, (dc in next dc, ch 1) twice, ★ work Cluster, ch 1, (dc in next dc, ch 1) twice, (3 dc, ch 3, 3 dc) in next ch-3 sp, ch 1, skip next 2 dc, (dc in next dc, ch 1) twice; repeat from ★ across to last 2 dc, work ending decrease.

8

To work decrease, YO, insert hook in next dc, YO and pull up a loop, YO and draw through 2 loops on hook, ★ YO, skip **next** ch-1 sp, insert hook in **next** st, YO and pull up a loop, YO and draw through 2 loops on hook; repeat from ★ once **more**, YO and draw through all 4 loops on hook.

Row 3: Ch 2, turn; skip first st, (dc in next dc, ch 1) 3 times, (3 dc, ch 3, 3 dc) in next ch-3 sp, ch 1, skip next 2 dc, (dc in next dc, ch 1) twice, ★ decrease, ch 1, (dc in next dc, ch 1) twice, (3 dc, ch 3, 3 dc) in next ch-3 sp, ch 1, skip next 2 dc, (dc in next dc, ch 1) twice; repeat from ★ across to last 2 dc, work ending decrease.

Repeat Rows 2 and 3 until Afghan measures approximately 44" from beginning ch, ending by working Row 3; do **not** finish off.

EDGING

Ch 2, do **not** turn; dc in top of last st on last row; working in end of rows, skip first row, (slip st, ch 2, dc) in top of next row and each row across; working in free loops of beginning ch *(Fig. 10, page 23)*, (slip st, ch 3, slip st, ch 1, hdc) in first ch, skip next ch, [(slip st, ch 1, hdc) in next ch, skip next ch] 3 times, slip st in next ch, [(slip st, ch 1, hdc) in next ch, skip next ch] 4 times, ★ (slip st, ch 3, slip st, ch 1, hdc) in next ch, skip next ch, [(slip st, ch 1, hdc) in next ch, skip next ch] 3 times, slip st in next ch, [(slip st, ch 1, hdc) in next ch, skip next ch] 4 times; repeat from ★ 9 times **more**, (slip st, ch 3, slip st, ch 2, dc) in next ch; working in end of rows, (slip st, ch 2, dc) in top of each row across to last row, skip last row; working in sts and in sps on last row, (slip st, ch 1, hdc) in first dc, (slip st, ch 1, hdc) in next 3 ch-1 sps, skip next dc, (slip st, ch 1, hdc) in next dc, (slip st, ch 3, slip st, ch 1, hdc) in next ch-3 sp, skip next dc, (slip st, ch 1, hdc) in next dc, † (slip st, ch 1, hdc) in next 2 ch-1 sps, slip st in next ch-1 sp and in next st, (slip st, ch 1, hdc) in next 3 ch-1 sps, skip next dc, (slip st, ch 1, hdc) in next dc, (slip st, ch 3, slip st, ch 1, hdc) in next ch-3 sp, skip next dc, (slip st, ch 1, hdc) in next dc †, repeat from † to † 9 times **more**, (slip st, ch 1, hdc) in last 3 sps; join with slip st to st at base of beginning ch-2, finish off.

Design by Anne Halliday.

3. RICKRACK CHARMER

Shown on page 26.

Finished Size:
35" x 44"

MATERIALS
Sport Weight Yarn:
Solid Only
16½ ounces,
(470 grams, 1,555 yards)
Multi-Colored Only
Green - 6 ounces,
(170 grams, 565 yards)
White - 5¼ ounces,
(150 grams, 495 yards)
Pink - 5¼ ounces,
(150 grams, 495 yards)
Crochet hook, size F (3.75 mm)
or size needed for gauge

GAUGE: In pattern, 19 sts (from point to point) = 2½";
7 rows = 4"

MULTI-COLORED ONLY
Stripe Sequence: One row **each** color *(Fig. 8, page 23)*: Green, ★ Pink, White, Green; repeat from ★ 24 times **more**.

AFGHAN BODY
Ch 229 **loosely**.

Row 1 (Right side)**:** Dc in sixth ch from hook, ch 1, skip next ch, (dc in next ch, ch 1, skip next ch) twice, (dc, ch 1) 4 times in next ch, skip next ch, dc in next ch, (ch 1, skip next ch, dc in next ch) twice, ★ skip next 3 chs, (dc in next ch, ch 1, skip next ch) 3 times, (dc, ch 1) 4 times in next ch, skip next ch, dc in next ch, (ch 1, skip next ch, dc in next ch) twice; repeat from ★ across to last 3 chs, skip next 2 chs, dc in last ch: 141 dc and 126 ch-1 sps.

Note: Mark last row as **right** side.

Row 2: Ch 3 **(counts as first dc, now and throughout)**, turn; skip first ch-1 sp, dc in next ch-1 sp, (ch 1, dc in next ch-1 sp) twice, (ch 1, dc) 4 times in next ch-1 sp, (ch 1, dc in next ch-1 sp) 3 times, ★ skip next 2 ch-1 sps, dc in next ch-1 sp, (ch 1, dc in next ch-1 sp) twice, (ch 1, dc) 4 times in next ch-1 sp, (ch 1, dc in next ch-1 sp) 3 times; repeat from ★ across to last 2 dc, skip last 2 dc, dc in next ch: 142 dc and 126 ch-1 sps.

Rows 3-76: Ch 3, turn; skip first ch-1 sp, dc in next ch-1 sp, (ch 1, dc in next ch-1 sp) twice, (ch 1, dc) 4 times in next ch-1 sp, (ch 1, dc in next ch-1 sp) 3 times, ★ skip next 2 ch-1 sps, dc in next ch-1 sp, (ch 1, dc in next ch-1 sp) twice, (ch 1, dc) 4 times in next ch-1 sp, (ch 1, dc in next ch-1 sp) 3 times; repeat from ★ across to last 3 dc, skip next 2 dc, dc in last dc.

Solid ONLY: Do not finish off.

Multi-Colored ONLY: Finish off.

EDGING

To work Picot, ch 3, sc in third ch from hook.

SOLID ONLY

Turn; slip st in first 2 dc and in next ch-1 sp, ch 1, sc in same sp, [(work Picot, sc in next ch-1 sp) 8 times, skip next 2 dc, sc in next ch-1 sp] 13 times, work Picot, (sc in next ch-1 sp, work Picot) 8 times; working in end of rows, (sc, work Picot, sc) in each row across to last row, (sc, work Picot) 3 times in last row; working over beginning ch, (sc, work Picot) in next 2 ch-1 sps, sc in next 2 ch-1 sps, work Picot, (sc in next ch-1 sp, work Picot) twice, ★ (sc, work Picot) twice in next ch-3 sp, (sc in next ch-1 sp, work Picot) twice, sc in next 2 ch-1 sps, work Picot, (sc in next ch-1 sp, work Picot) twice; repeat from ★ 12 times **more**, sc in next sp, (work Picot, sc in same sp) twice; working in end of rows, (sc, work Picot, sc) in next row and in each row across to last row, (sc, work Picot) twice in last row; join with slip st to first sc, finish off.

MULTI-COLORED ONLY

With **right** side facing, join White with sc in first ch-1 sp on Row 76 *(see Joining With Sc, page 23)*; [(work Picot, sc in next ch-1 sp) 8 times, skip next 2 dc, sc in next ch-1 sp] 13 times, work Picot, (sc in next ch-1 sp, work Picot) 8 times; working in end of rows, (sc, work Picot, sc) in each row across to last row, (sc, work Picot) 3 times in last row; working over beginning ch, (sc, work Picot) in next 2 ch-1 sps, sc in next 2 ch-1 sps, work Picot, (sc in next ch-1 sp, work Picot) twice, ★ (sc, work Picot) twice in next ch-3 sp, (sc in next ch-1 sp, work Picot) twice, sc in next 2 ch-1 sps, work Picot, (sc in next ch-1 sp, work Picot) twice; repeat from ★ 12 times **more**, sc in next sp, (work Picot, sc in same sp) twice; working in end of rows, (sc, work Picot, sc) in next row and in each row across to last row, (sc, work Picot) twice in last row; join with slip st to first sc, finish off.

Design by Terry Kimbrough.

11

4. TUTTI-FRUTTI PARFAIT

Shown on page 24.

Finished Size:
38" x 46"

MATERIALS

Worsted Weight Brushed Acrylic Yarn:
White - 10 ounces,
(280 grams, 770 yards)
Mint - 3 ounces,
(90 grams, 230 yards)
Blue - 3 ounces,
(90 grams, 230 yards)
Yellow - 3 ounces,
(90 grams, 230 yards)
Peach - 3 ounces,
(90 grams, 230 yards)
Crochet hook, size H (5.00 mm)
or size needed for gauge

GAUGE: In pattern,
2 repeats (from point to point)
and 8 rows = 5"

STRIPE SEQUENCE

One row of **each** color: Mint *(Fig. 8, page 23)*, ★ White, Blue, White, Yellow, White, Peach, White, Mint; repeat from ★ 8 times **more**.

AFGHAN

To work V-St, (dc, ch 1, dc) in st indicated.

To work Shell, dc in st indicated, (ch 1, dc in same st) twice.

To work Cluster (uses next 5 sps and sts), YO, insert hook in next ch-1 sp, YO and pull up a loop, YO and draw through 2 loops on hook, ★ YO, skip **next** dc, insert hook in **next** st or sp, YO and pull up a loop, YO and draw through 2 loops on hook; repeat from ★ once **more**, YO and draw through all 4 loops on hook.

To work ending Cluster (uses last 3 sts), ★ YO, insert hook in **next** st or sp, YO and pull up a loop, YO and draw through 2 loops on hook; repeat from ★ 2 times **more**, YO and draw through all 4 loops on hook.

With Mint, ch 182 **loosely**.

Row 1 (Right side)**:** YO, insert hook in third ch from hook, YO and pull up a loop, YO and draw through 2 loops on hook, YO, insert hook in next ch, YO and pull up a loop, YO and draw through 2 loops on hook, YO and draw through all 3 loops on hook, skip next ch, work V-St in next ch, skip next ch, work Shell in next ch, skip next ch, work

V-St in next ch, ★ (YO, skip next ch, insert hook in next ch, YO and pull up a loop, YO and draw through 2 loops on hook) 3 times, YO and draw through all 4 loops on hook, skip next ch, work V-St in next ch, skip next ch, work Shell in next ch, skip next ch, work V-St in next ch; repeat from ★ across to last 4 chs, skip next ch, work ending Cluster: 105 dc.

Note: Mark last row as **right** side.

To work decrease (uses next 2 sts or sps), ★ YO, insert hook in **next** st or sp, YO and pull up a loop, YO and draw through 2 loops on hook; repeat from ★ once **more**, YO and draw through all 3 loops on hook.

Rows 2-73: Ch 2, turn; decrease, skip next dc, work V-St in next dc, skip next ch-1 sp, work Shell in next dc, skip next ch-1 sp, work V-St in next dc, ★ skip next dc, work Cluster, skip next dc, work V-St in next dc, skip next ch-1 sp, work Shell in next dc, skip next ch-1 sp, work V-St in next dc; repeat from ★ across to last ch-1 sp, skip next dc, work ending Cluster.

Finish off.

Design by Carole Prior.

---

5. RIBBON CANDY

Shown on page 2.

Finished Size:
28" x 39"

MATERIALS
Baby Fingering Weight Yarn:
White - 3¹/₂ ounces,
(100 grams, 500 yards)
Pink - 1¹/₂ ounces,
(40 grams, 215 yards)
Peach - 1¹/₂ ounces,
(40 grams, 215 yards)
Yellow - 1¹/₂ ounces,
(40 grams, 215 yards)

Mint - 1¹/₂ ounces,
(40 grams, 215 yards)
Blue - 1¹/₂ ounces,
(40 grams, 215 yards)
Crochet hook, size D (3.00 mm)
or size needed for gauge

GAUGE: In pattern, 30 sts and 15 rows = 5"

AFGHAN BODY

With Pink, ch 168 **loosely**.

Row 1: 2 Dc in fourth ch from hook, dc in next 5 chs, skip next 2 chs, dc in next 6 chs, ★ 3 dc in next ch, dc in next 6 chs, skip next 2 chs, dc in next 6 chs; repeat from ★ across to last ch, 2 dc in last ch: 166 sts.

Row 2 (Right side)**:** Ch 3 (counts as first dc, now and throughout), turn; working in Back Loops Only *(Fig. 9, page 23)*, 2 dc in next dc, dc in next 5 dc, skip next 2 dc, dc in next 6 dc, ★ 3 dc in next dc, dc in next 6 dc, skip next 2 dc, dc in next 6 dc; repeat from ★ across to last st, 2 dc in last st.

Note: Mark last row as **right** side.

Row 3: Repeat Row 2; finish off.

Row 4: With **right** side facing and working in both loops, join White with slip st in first dc; slip st in each dc across, changing to Peach in last slip st *(Fig. 8, page 23)*.

Row 5: Ch 3, turn; working in Back Loops Only of dc one row **below** slip sts, 2 dc in next dc, dc in next 5 dc, skip next 2 dc, dc in next 6 dc, ★ 3 dc in next dc, dc in next 6 dc, skip next 2 dc, dc in next 6 dc; repeat from ★ across to last dc, 2 dc in last dc.

Rows 6 and 7: Repeat Row 2 twice; at the end of Row 7, finish off.

Row 8: Repeat Row 4, changing to Yellow in last slip st.

Rows 9-11: Repeat Rows 5-7.

Row 12: Repeat Row 4, changing to Mint in last slip st.

Rows 13-15: Repeat Rows 5-7.

Row 16: Repeat Row 4, changing to Blue in last slip st.

Rows 17-19: Repeat Rows 5-7.

Row 20: With **right** side facing and working in both loops, join White with slip st in first dc; slip st in each dc across.

Rows 21-23: Repeat Rows 5-7.

Row 24: With Pink, repeat Row 4, changing to White in last slip st.

Rows 25-27: Repeat Rows 5-7.

Row 28: With Peach, repeat Row 4, changing to White in last slip st.

Rows 29-31: Repeat Rows 5-7.

Row 32: With Yellow, repeat Row 4, changing to White in last slip st.

Rows 33-35: Repeat Rows 5-7.

Row 36: With Mint, repeat Row 4, changing to White in last slip st.

Rows 37-39: Repeat Rows 5-7.

Row 40: With Blue, repeat Row 4, changing to Pink in last slip st.

Rows 41-43: Repeat Rows 5-7.

Rows 44-60: Repeat Rows 4-20, changing to Mint in last slip st of Row 60.

Rows 61-63: Repeat Rows 5-7.

Row 64: Repeat Row 4, changing to Yellow in last slip st.

Rows 65-67: Repeat Rows 5-7.

Row 68: Repeat Row 4, changing to Peach in last slip st.

Rows 69-71: Repeat Rows 5-7.

Row 72: Repeat Row 4, changing to Pink in last slip st.

Rows 73-75: Repeat Rows 5-7.

Row 76: With Blue, repeat Row 4, changing to White in last slip st.

Rows 77-79: Repeat Rows 5-7.

Row 80: With Mint, repeat Row 4, changing to White in last slip st.

Rows 81-83: Repeat Rows 5-7.

Row 84: With Yellow, repeat Row 4, changing to White in last slip st.

Rows 85-87: Repeat Rows 5-7.

Row 88: With Peach, repeat Row 4, changing to White in last slip st.

Rows 89-91: Repeat Rows 5-7.

Row 92: With Pink, repeat Row 4, changing to White in last slip st.

Rows 93-95: Repeat Rows 5-7; at the end of Row 95, do **not** finish off.

Row 96: Turn; working in both loops, slip st in each dc across, changing to Blue in last slip st.

Rows 97-99: Repeat Rows 5-7.

Row 100: Repeat Row 4, changing to Mint in last slip st.

Rows 101-103: Repeat Rows 5-7.

Row 104: Repeat Row 4, changing to Yellow in last slip st.

Rows 105-107: Repeat Rows 5-7.

Row 108: Repeat Row 4, changing to Peach in last slip st.

Rows 109-111: Repeat Rows 5-7.

Row 112: Repeat Row 4, changing to Pink in last slip st.

Rows 113-115: Repeat Rows 5-7; at the end of Row 115, do **not** finish off.

EDGING
TOP
Ch 1, turn; 2 sc in first dc, sc in next 6 dc, skip next 2 dc, sc in next 6 dc, ★ 3 sc in next dc, sc in next 6 dc, skip next 2 dc, sc in next 6 dc; repeat from ★ across to last dc, 2 sc in last dc, finish off.

BOTTOM
With **right** side facing and working in free loops of beginning ch *(Fig. 10, page 23)*, join Pink with slip st in first ch; ch 1, pull up a loop in each of first 2 chs, YO and draw through all 3 loops on hook, sc in next 5 chs, 3 sc in next ch-2 sp, sc in next 5 chs, ★ skip next 3 chs, sc in next 5 chs, 3 sc in next ch-2 sp, sc in next 5 chs; repeat from ★ across to last 2 chs, pull up a loop in each of last 2 chs, YO and draw through all 3 loops on hook, finish off.

Design by Rose Marie Brooks.

6. SEAFOAM WAVES
Shown on page 3.

Finished Size:
32½" x 44"

MATERIALS
Sport Weight Yarn:
Green - 7½ ounces,
(210 grams, 600 yards)
White - 4½ ounces,
(130 grams, 360 yards)
Blue - 4 ounces,
(110 grams, 320 yards)
Crochet hook, size F (3.75 mm)
or size needed for gauge

GAUGE: In pattern, (from point to point) = 2½"; 7 rows = 3¾"

AFGHAN
With White, ch 213 **loosely**.

Row 1: Dc in fifth ch from hook, ★ † ch 1, (skip next ch, dc in next ch, ch 1) twice, [YO, skip next ch, insert hook in next ch, YO and pull up a loop, YO and draw through 2 loops on hook, YO, skip next 3 chs, insert hook in next ch, YO and pull up a loop, YO and draw through 2 loops on hook, YO and draw through all 3 loops on

16

hook **(counts as one dc)]**, ch 1, (skip next ch, dc in next ch, ch 1) twice, skip next ch †, (dc, ch 3, dc) in next ch; repeat from ★ 11 times **more**, then repeat from † to † once, (dc, ch 1, dc) in last ch: 92 dc and 92 sps.

To work decrease (uses next 3 dc), YO, insert hook in next dc, YO and pull up a loop, YO and draw through 2 loops on hook, YO, skip next dc, insert hook in next dc, YO and pull up a loop, YO and draw through 2 loops on hook, YO and draw through all 3 loops on hook **(counts as one dc)**.

Row 2 (Right side)**:** Ch 4 **(counts as first dc plus ch 1, now and throughout)**, turn; dc in same st, ch 1, (dc in next dc, ch 1) twice, decrease, ch 1, (dc in next dc, ch 1) twice, ★ (dc, ch 3, dc) in next ch-3 sp, ch 1, (dc in next dc, ch 1) twice, decrease, ch 1, (dc in next dc, ch 1) twice; repeat from ★ across to last sp, skip next ch, (dc, ch 1, dc) in next ch changing to Green in last dc *(Fig. 8, page 23)*: 93 dc and 92 sps.

Note: Mark last row as **right** side.

Row 3: Ch 4, turn; dc in same st, ch 1, (dc in next dc, ch 1) twice, decrease, ch 1, (dc in next dc, ch 1) twice, ★ (dc, ch 3, dc) in next ch-3 sp, ch 1, (dc in next dc, ch 1) twice, decrease, ch 1, (dc in next dc, ch 1) twice; repeat from ★ across to last dc, (dc, ch 1, dc) in last dc.

Row 4: Ch 4, turn; dc in same st, ch 1, (dc in next dc, ch 1) twice, decrease, ch 1, (dc in next dc, ch 1) twice, ★ (dc, ch 3, dc) in next ch-3 sp, ch 1, (dc in next dc, ch 1) twice, decrease, ch 1, (dc in next dc, ch 1) twice; repeat from ★ across to last dc, (dc, ch 1, dc) in last dc changing to Blue in last dc.

Rows 5 and 6: Repeat Rows 3 and 4 changing to Green at end of last row.

Rows 7 and 8: Repeat Rows 3 and 4 changing to White at end of last row.

Rows 9 and 10: Repeat Rows 3 and 4 changing to Green at end of last row.

Rows 11-80: Repeat Rows 3-10, 8 times; then repeat Rows 3-8 once **more**.

Rows 81 and 82: Ch 4, turn; dc in same st, ch 1, (dc in next dc, ch 1) twice, decrease, ch 1, (dc in next dc, ch 1) twice, ★ (dc, ch 3, dc) in next ch-3 sp, ch 1, (dc in next dc, ch 1) twice, decrease, ch 1, (dc in next dc, ch 1) twice; repeat from ★ across to last dc, (dc, ch 1, dc) in last dc.

Finish off.

Design by Melissa Leapman.

7. ICICLE DREAMS

Shown on page 25.

Finished Size:
35" x 42"

MATERIALS
Worsted Weight Brushed Acrylic Yarn:
White - 12 ounces,
(340 grams, 925 yards)
Blue - 11 ounces,
(310 grams, 850 yards)
Crochet hook, size I (5.50 mm) **or** size needed for gauge

GAUGE: 37 sts (from point to point) = 7" and 12 rows = 4"

STRIPE SEQUENCE
Work 4 rows of **each** color **(Fig. 8, page 23)**: ★ White, Blue; repeat from ★ throughout, ending by working 2 rows of White.

AFGHAN
With White, ch 184 **loosely**.

Row 1: Sc in second ch from hook and in next 16 chs, 3 sc in next ch, sc in next 17 chs, (skip next 2 chs, sc in next 17 chs, 3 sc in next ch, sc in next 17 chs) across: 185 sc.

Rows 2-4: Ch 1, turn; skip first sc, sc in next 17 sc, 3 sc in next sc, ★ sc in next 17 sc, skip next 2 sc, sc in next 17 sc, 3 sc in next sc; repeat from ★ 3 times **more**, sc in next 16 sc, skip next sc, sc in last sc.

To work Long double crochet (abbreviated Ldc), YO, insert hook in next st 2 rows **below**, YO and pull up a loop even with last st made, (YO and draw through 2 loops on hook) twice.

To work extended Long double crochet (abbreviated ex Ldc), YO, insert hook in next st 3 rows **below**, YO and pull up a loop even with last st made, (YO and draw through 2 loops on hook) twice.

Row 5: Ch 1, turn; skip first sc, sc in next 2 sc, work Ldc, (sc in next sc, work ex Ldc, sc in next sc, work Ldc) 3 times, sc in next 2 sc, 3 sc in next sc, sc in next 2 sc, work Ldc, sc in next sc, (work ex Ldc, sc in next sc, work Ldc, sc in next sc) 3 times, ★ work ex Ldc, skip next 2 sc, work ex Ldc, sc in next sc, work Ldc, (sc in next sc, work ex Ldc, sc in next sc, work Ldc) 3 times, sc in next 2 sc, 3 sc in next sc, sc in next 2 sc, work Ldc, sc in next sc, (work ex Ldc, sc in next sc, work Ldc, sc in next sc) 3 times; repeat from ★ across to last 2 sc, skip next sc, sc in last sc.

Rows 6-8: Ch 1, turn; skip first sc, sc in next 17 sts, 3 sc in next sc, ★ sc in next 17 sts, skip next 2 sts, sc in next 17 sts, 3 sc in next sc; repeat from ★ 3 times **more**, sc in next 16 sts, skip next sc, sc in last sc.

Rows 9-122: Repeat Rows 5-8, 28 times; then repeat Rows 5 and 6 once **more**.

Finish off.

Design by Carole Prior.

---

8. FEATHERY LACE
Shown on page 1.

Finished Size:
38½" x 52"

MATERIALS
Sport Weight Yarn:
20 ounces,
(570 grams, 2,000 yards)
Crochet hook, size H (5.00 mm) **or** size needed for gauge

GAUGE: 16 hdc and 12 rows = 4"

AFGHAN
Ch 155 **loosely**.

Row 1 (Right side)**:** Hdc in third ch from hook and in each ch across: 154 sts.

Note: Mark last row as **right** side.

To work hdc decrease (uses next 3 hdc), YO, insert hook in next hdc, YO and pull up a loop, YO, skip next hdc, insert hook in next hdc, YO and pull up a loop, YO and draw through all 5 loops on hook **(counts as one hdc)**.

Row 2: Ch 2 **(counts as first hdc, now and throughout)**, turn; hdc in next 8 hdc, hdc decrease, ★ hdc in next 7 hdc, 2 hdc in each of next 2 hdc, hdc in next 7 hdc, hdc decrease; repeat from ★ across to last 9 sts, hdc in last 9 sts: 152 hdc.

Row 3: Ch 2, turn; hdc in next hdc and in each hdc across.

To work treble crochet (abbreviated tr), YO twice, insert hook in st indicated, YO and pull up a loop (4 loops on hook), (YO and draw through 2 loops on hook) 3 times *(Figs. 7a & b, page 23)*.

To work tr decrease, YO twice, insert hook in next hdc, YO and pull up a loop, (YO and draw through 2 loops on hook) twice, YO twice, skip next hdc, insert hook in next hdc, YO and pull up a loop, (YO and draw through 2 loops on hook) twice, YO and draw through all 3 loops on hook **(counts as one tr)**.

19

Row 4: Ch 5 (counts as first tr plus ch 1), turn; (tr, ch 1) twice in same st, ★ † (skip next hdc, tr in next hdc) 3 times, skip next hdc, tr decrease, (skip next hdc, tr in next hdc) 3 times, skip next hdc, (ch 1, tr) 3 times in next hdc †, (tr, ch 1) 3 times in next hdc; repeat from ★ 6 times **more**, then repeat from † to † once: 104 tr.

Row 5: Ch 2, turn; hdc in same tr and in each ch and tr across to last tr, 2 hdc in last tr: 154 hdc.

Repeat Rows 2-5 until Afghan measures approximately 52" from beginning ch, ending by working Row 3.

Finish off.

Design by Carole Tippett.

GENERAL INSTRUCTIONS

ABBREVIATIONS

ch(s)	chain(s)
dc	double crochet(s)
hdc	half double crochet(s)
ex Ldc	extended long double crochet(s)
Ldc	long double crochet(s)
mm	millimeters
sc	single crochet(s)
sp(s)	space(s)
st(s)	stitch(es)
tr	treble crochet(s)
YO	yarn over

★ — work instructions following ★ as many more times as indicated in addition to the first time.

† to † — work all instructions from first † to second † **as many** times as specified.

( ) or [ ] — work enclosed instructions **as many** times as specified by the number immediately following **or** work all enclosed instructions in the stitch or space indicated **or** contains explanatory remarks.

CROCHET TERMINOLOGY	
UNITED STATES	**INTERNATIONAL**
slip stitch (slip st) =	single crochet (sc)
single crochet (sc) =	double crochet (dc)
half double crochet (hdc) =	half treble crochet (htr)
double crochet (dc) =	treble crochet (tr)
treble crochet (tr) =	double treble crochet (dtr)
double treble crochet (dtr) =	triple treble crochet (ttr)
skip =	miss

ALUMINUM CROCHET HOOKS	
UNITED STATES	METRIC (mm)
B-1	2.25
C-2	2.75
D-3	3.25
E-4	3.50
F-5	3.75
G-6	4.00
H-8	5.00
I-9	5.50
J-10	6.00
K-10½	6.50
N	9.00
P	10.00
Q	15.00

GAUGE

Exact gauge is **essential** for proper size. Before beginning your project, make a sample swatch approximately 4" square in the stitch, yarn, and hook specified. If your swatch is larger or smaller than specified, **make another, changing hook size to get the correct gauge**. Keep trying until you find the size hook that will give you the specified gauge.

CHAIN

To work a chain stitch, begin with a slip knot on the hook. Bring the yarn **over** hook from back to front, catching the yarn with the hook and turning the hook slightly toward you to keep the yarn from slipping off. Draw the yarn through the slip knot **(Fig. 1) (first chain st made, abbreviated ch)**.

Fig. 1

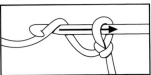

WORKING INTO THE CHAIN

When counting chains, always begin with the first chain from the hook and then count toward the beginning of your foundation chain **(Fig. 2a)**.

Fig. 2a

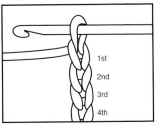

1st
2nd
3rd
4th

Method 1: Insert hook under top two strands of each chain **(Fig. 2b)**.

Fig. 2b

Method 2: Insert hook into back ridge of each chain *(Fig. 2c)*.

Fig. 2c

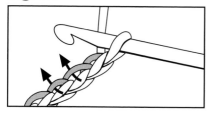

SLIP STITCH

To work a slip stitch, insert hook in st or sp indicated, YO and draw through st and through loop on hook *(Fig. 3)* **(slip stitch made,** *abbreviated slip st)*.

Fig. 3

SINGLE CROCHET

Insert hook in st or sp indicated, YO and pull up a loop, YO and draw through both loops on hook *(Fig. 4)* **(single crochet made,** *abbreviated sc)*.

Fig. 4

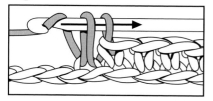

HALF DOUBLE CROCHET

YO, insert hook in st or sp indicated, YO and pull up a loop, YO and draw through all 3 loops on hook *(Fig. 5)* **(half double crochet made,** *abbreviated hdc)*.

Fig. 5

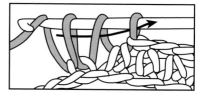

DOUBLE CROCHET

YO, insert hook in st or sp indicated, YO and pull up a loop (3 loops on hook), YO and draw through 2 loops on hook *(Fig. 6a)*, YO and draw through remaining 2 loops on hook *(Fig. 6b)* **(double crochet made,** *abbreviated dc)*.

Fig. 6a

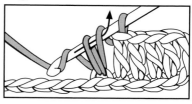

Fig. 6b

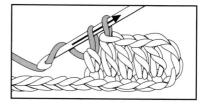

TREBLE CROCHET

YO twice, insert hook in st or sp indicated, YO and pull up a loop (4 loops on hook) *(Fig. 7a)*, (YO and draw through 2 loops on hook) 3 times *(Fig. 7b)* (treble crochet made, *abbreviated tr)*.

Fig. 7a

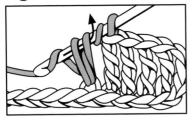

Fig. 7b

JOINING WITH SC

When instructed to join with sc, begin with a slip knot on hook. Insert hook in st or sp indicated, YO and pull up a loop, YO and draw through both loops on hook.

CHANGING COLORS

Work the last stitch to within one step of completion, hook new yarn *(Fig. 8)* and draw through all loops on hook. Cut old yarn and work over both ends.

Fig. 8

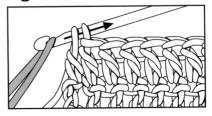

BACK OR FRONT LOOP ONLY

Work only in loop(s) indicated by arrow *(Fig. 9)*.

Fig. 9

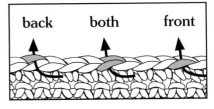

back   both   front

FREE LOOPS OF A CHAIN

When instructed to work in free loops of a chain, work in loop indicated by arrow *(Fig. 10)*.

Fig. 10

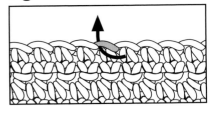

We have made every effort to ensure that these instructions are accurate and complete. We cannot, however, be responsible for human error, typographical mistakes, or variations in individual work.

4

Give Baby a triple treat with this dreamy confection featuring three pretty stitches in brushed acrylic worsted weight yarn.

Reminiscent of icicles, extended stitches add a wintry look to this cozy wrap.